The Healing

Hans-Werner Schroeder

The Healing Power of Prayer

Translated and revised by Jon Madsen

Floris Books

First published in German as *Die Heilkraft des Gebetes*
in 1991 by Verein für ein erweitertes Heilwesen

First published in 1991 by the Sydney Centre of The
Christain Community in Australia

This edition published in 2008 by Floris Books
© 1991 Verein für ein erweitertes Heilwesen e. V.
Bad Liebenzell-Unterlengenhardt

British Library CIP Data available

ISBN 978-086315-624-3

Printed in Poland

Contents

Why Pray?   7

  Loss of equilibrium   8

  Not too fast!   9

  Success?   11

  Peace   12

  Constructive Forces   17

  Living in the World   19

Prayer is no longer a matter of course   20

  Origin and foundation of life   22

  Egoism in Prayer   24

  Intercession   25

The Lord's Prayer   28

  A classic example   30

  The Lord's Prayer, continuation   32

  Is our prayer heard?   35

  Peace, trust, love, thankfulness   38

The Healing Power of Prayer   41

  Sleeping and waking   44

  Healing of the soul and healing of the body   47

  Constancy   49

Particular Forms of Prayer   52

  For the dead   52

  For the sick   54

  For children   56

  Grace before meals   56

  Prayer when in distress   57

  Conclusion   58

Verses and Prayers   60

Recommended Reading   61

Why Pray?

In recent years cases of cancer, heart and metabolic diseases, as well as allergies of every kind, have been increasing in frequency — and these are only some of the complaints threatening the *physical* health of human beings. In addition to this, also growing at an alarming rate, there are diseases and dangers which originate in the sphere of *soul* and *spirit*. It is not just that we have learned to recognize clearly the *soul-related* part of many diseases — the so-called psychosomatic illnesses, in which our inner attitudes and frailties of soul and spirit can trigger and worsen the physical symptoms; we have also become ever more aware of such other dangers as alcohol and nicotine dependence, drug addiction, depression and phobias, all of which add to the rising incidence of "mental illnesses" like schizophrenia and schizoid conditions. All of these problems can seem like an avalanche threatening to engulf us; their connection to problems of the soul and spirit seem very clear.

With all this in mind, it seems appropriate to seek for remedies that may bring healing for the soul and spirit. One activity with a great potential for healing is *prayer.* Initially, let us just use the word 'prayer' in a quite general sense to mean: any human effort which aims to make the soul more harmonious and 'inward.' In its more precise meaning, of course, prayer is the foundation of all *religious* life — we shall look at this in more detail later. But even if we do not have and are not looking for a religious approach to life we may, in some situations — bereavement, say, or the shock of a sudden serious illness — feel the need to look for a source of inner peace; perhaps we may even find that we want to 'look up' and turn to something greater than ourselves. Such endeavours also call upon powers within us which can help to restore the health of soul and spirit.

It is the aim of this little book to describe ways and means of promoting inner harmony and peace, to help you in such attempts to look up and turn to something greater.

Loss of equilibrium

In today's world we find ourselves pushed ever more deeply into materialism, and it is no longer easy to gain access to the sources of peace, reflection and contemplation.

Most of us find ourselves unable to avoid living conditions that rob us of our inner balance. Stress, restlessness and haste seem unavoidable, due to the demands of everyday life. And even in our homes — which we may think of as havens of rest and relaxation — images and reports of events from all over the world are delivered to us, putting us under strain, often worrying and even frightening us.

There is no point in deploring all this. It is a fact and a condition of our life today, though a first step towards a more conscious relationship to ourselves and our surroundings could be to decide for ourselves not simply to go along with and join in everything that comes upon us from outside.

There is no need to join in and go along with everything that comes at us!

But it is even more profitable to ask what possibilities there might be for balancing or even healing the one-sidedness of our life.

So let us consider instead a particular outcome of one-sided materialism, namely the danger that we may lose our 'inner equilibrium.' This metaphor implies that, to a dangerous degree, we are being deprived of inner uprightness; in the absence of inner 'balance,' we are in danger of 'falling.'

But the other, hopeful, aspect of this image is that the balance may be restored — as with a pair of scales — by adding 'weight' to the side that is too light.

Do not neglect that other side of the scales — it can restore the equilibrium!

So we can say to ourselves: 'What could balance the scales? I will seriously and thoroughly examine my store of soul forces and consider what I can and must do for the sake of the balance of my soul, for my inner health. This is my starting point: in the midst of the unrest in my life, I shall look for ways of creating moments of reflection and peace, within and without. I shall strive to fill these moments with thoughts and feelings that can give me inner strength and keep me upright.'

Not too fast!

One may now be thinking: 'I don't have time for such moments of peace and reflection.' On closer examination, though, this objection will often turn out to be no more than a (more or less subtle!) excuse to avoid the inner effort that we know will be needed. To face up to this objection, just consider this: we are normally awake for approximately 16 hours a day. These 16 hours contain roughly 1000 minutes. Now is it really a fact that, of these 1000 minutes, we cannot spare 5 minutes a day to throw into the scales, in order to counterbalance the 995 other minutes? It seems hard to believe!

Of course, creating a free space every day will, initially, require some energy and a certain amount of *planning*.

- The very first question is: when, during the course of the day, is the best time to establish these moments of stillness? For many people *evening* will be the only possible time, when the activities of the day have come to their natural conclusion. Others will be too tired at night and will find *morning* the appropriate time, drawing peace from the lingering quiet of the night. You should try what is best for *you;* there are often other suitable moments in the course of the day.

- When we first begin to take our inner life in hand, we often make the mistake of attempting too much in one go. To avoid this, try

9

the following: having thoroughly considered and assessed all possibilities, set aside just a short period of time at first, no more than three to five minutes a day, say — but then stick strictly to this plan for a time. Experience shows that it is best to make a commitment for a limited time — a number of days or weeks, for example.

• So we might say: I shall set aside three to five minutes a day — if possible at the same time every day — for quiet contemplation, and it is my intention to keep this up for, say, two weeks. At the end of these two weeks I shall look back and ask: how have I fared during this time? Does it work at the time I chose, or do I need to change it? Have I managed to come to grips at all with the task I set myself? Should I continue in the same way, or should I perhaps change course? Are even three to five minutes too long for me — and they can seem very 'long' if one lacks practice! — or do I feel strong enough to ask more of myself? Could I manage a second moment of stillness in the morning (or evening)?

• In short: when we have honestly and sincerely worked through the prescribed period, we are again *free* to make the decision *anew* and to continue practising, but this time with the benefit of experience. As before, continue for a limited period of time and then repeat the exercise of reviewing, until eventually the experience and confidence gained will make such precautions unnecessary.

> *Everything begins small, and the greater and mightier it is to become, the more slowly and arduously it grows.*
> J.W. Goethe

Success?

The second obvious objection to the method suggested here is this: what use are just three to five minutes of reflection? That is not even enough for me to come to terms with my worries and my inner restlessness, let alone to allow anything meaningful to enter my soul!

> *To think well is to serve God in the interior court.*
> Thomas Traherne

We must not be too hasty in our judgment. In what we are attempting here, it is not important that we should be successful immediately. It is far more important that by persevering we begin to strengthen our inner resources, even if at first we don't *feel* as if we are making progress; this is more productive than it is to set out with great enthusiasm, only to give up again after a short time. Real and essential success comes from the *seeking* for peace and *learning to attain* it by consistent practice. This is, in itself, decisive for the inner growth of the soul.

Some people have made repeated attempts, only to abandon them after a short time; they were expecting too much, too soon. That is why we repeat the advice:

- To begin with, don't take on too much, and don't try to exercise too long — but keep with it!

- Ever and again re-establish inner freedom by reviewing and gathering new impetus for the next stretch of the journey! This will slowly strengthen the forces of the soul to the point where the moments of contemplation can be extended and lived through more profoundly.

- Here is something else we should be aware of: at first — because everything is new and therefore interesting — we may feel a certain gratification which helps to cope with any initial problems we encounter. This pleasurable feeling will evaporate after a certain time as the initial enthusiasm wanes. From then on, more of our *own* energy is required to keep us going. We should know that this waning is not solely due to our own inner weakness. We are encountering a spiritual law, which applies to all honest spiritual work: sincerely striving human beings must be allowed to live by *their own* resources and *their own* power of decision. After all, it is only through this greater challenge that they have the real chance of achieving the necessary enhancement of their inner energies.

We may, no doubt, find that even the very first steps on the path suggested here will be quite difficult; and then there is a danger that, having failed a few times, we lose heart. *Nothing could be more misguided!* The very fact that our first efforts confront us with particular difficulties only shows how necessary it is to persevere. As soon as the realisation dawns that there really is no other way, we shall be able slowly to regain our inner balance. Now we can continue on our way, just as we would continue to take a bitter medicine, knowing that it was the only cure.

Peace

Very likely, the first difficulty we encounter will be that of *entering into* inner stillness. We have chosen a quiet time of day; now we may also find it helpful to choose a room that is relatively free from outside disturbances.

Begin with the body relaxed — but not limp! For some people, the quality of *lighting* is important: too much light, be it natural or artificial, may be found unhelpful, in which case it may be necessary to darken the room a little. In the evening, the light of a candle falling on an object that conveys stillness, such as a crystal, a flower or a picture, may help.

When all this has been arranged, there still remains the most decisive step: the creation of a state of *inner* calm. This is often more difficult than one might think, because it is just when the *exterior* situation is peaceful that our *inner* restlessness becomes all the more noticeable. Often, we discover that we have never really learned how to act in the absence of exterior stimuli. Normally, we are exposed all day long to every kind of demand, beginning with the alarm clock that jerks us awake, to the stress of the traffic on the way to work and the constant noise that is with us daily; in the evening there is reading to be done for professional reasons, or simply because the current book is "gripping", and then, of course, there is television; there is always something demanding or stimulating coming towards us from the world *outside*. But what happens when this constant flow of outer stimuli suddenly stops and we are completely alone with ourselves? Everyone has experienced the rush of thoughts and emotions that then threaten to swamp us and which are so hard to resist. Here, then, is the first task: to find real peace, deep peace! We are not used to this, nobody has taught us, and this is why the beginning itself is a challenge to be mastered.

Experience shows that the worst method is to try and 'press' stillness out of ourselves, as it were. That only gives rise to tension and further stress. We can try, as a first step, taking a few deep breaths. But then we can turn the soul in recollection towards moments in the past when we felt utterly at peace. These might be moments such as a calm, sunny day in the mountains or by the sea, a walk through the forest; the calm of evening after a hot summer's day; a sweet-smelling meadow under a cloudless sky; the overwhelming tranquillity of the star-studded night-sky ... the more concretely and distinctly we can make such experiences live again in our soul, the more deeply we shall be able to enter into their quality of stillness. For some people, looking at a work of art or remembering a few bars of music enables this stillness, this peace, to radiate towards them. Even the word 'peace' itself, repeated contemplatively several times, can engender in us something of its meaning.

We need to take our courage in both hands and experiment to find the starting point that is best for *us!* The main principle is simply this: to connect with an experience in which we felt still-ness and peace in as concentrated a way as possible. If we cannot think of any such experience, let us take the first opportunity that presents itself to create one — we will find it a great help in com-ing to rest, inwardly.

A starting point near at hand is this: the objects around us exude stillness. The table in front, the walls around us and the floor beneath, the chair on which we sit — none of them is hurried or restless; they are filled with profound stillness! Taking this into our consciousness allows this 'personified' stillness to work on us. We can open our eyes and see the table before us, feel its still-ness. Now, with closed eyes, 'breathe in' this stillness, as it were. As soon as this inner experience begins to fade, we can open our eyes again, refresh our perception of the table (or whatever object we have chosen) and then once more, with our eyes closed, absorb the stillness, allowing it to reverberate within. We can continue alternating between the experience of calm arising from the visual perception, and our own inner calm, until the inner calm has become strong enough.

We will find that the *recollection* of a powerful experience of peace, or the actual *immediate experience* via the senses can then help us to find the corresponding region of peace *within* ourselves; it is actually always present in us, although we mostly disregard it; nor is it always easy to reach it. By seeking out those experiences which convey peace to us from 'outside' — either as memories or as sense-experiences — we will be able, as it were, to 'breathe in' this peace and let it flow into us. But then we may also become aware of the deeper regions of our soul in which true peace reigns and which we can reach consciously in this way. The opening words of a meditation-text by Rudolf Steiner point to this spiritual truth:

Quiet I bear within me.
I bear within myself
forces that strengthen me.

Of course, most of us spend only a very small part of the day in that part of our being of which these words speak. But in this regard, human beings are rather like multi-storey buildings. With our consciousness we spend most of our time in the 'upper storey,' and from there it is not always easy to find the access, the 'stairs,' as it were, by which to descend into the deeper regions of our inner selves. Yet in these lower regions peace reigns supreme. The first challenge of the moments of contemplation is to reach these levels.

• When we begin to practise in this way, we may well find that the experience is variable from day to day; we may sometimes be quite successful in entering the stillness within. At other times, even the most strenuous efforts will fail to subdue our inner restlessness. We need to accept this with equanimity — not indifference — rather than be determined at all costs to achieve what, on this particular day, may just not be achievable. Better simply to abandon the attempt this time, knowing that we can try again tomorrow. If we are honest with ourselves, we will easily be able to tell whether we are giving up out of inner indolence, or because this time, try as we might, it just did not work.

Incidentally, lack of success in the evening is rarely due merely to lethargy or tiredness — just as failure in the morning rarely is down to insufficient sleep. We will be able to achieve far more than we initially think ourselves capable of if, instead of yielding to such external difficulties, we confront them head on. Apart from 'teething problems,' the occasional failure to achieve the experience of peace mostly has deep-seated causes which can be quite varied; sometimes they just have to be accepted.

At this point, let us take at least a passing look at two more steps we can take on our chosen path; they will be discussed further in due course.

Tranquillity can be *intensified.* When we have found real inner tranquillity, something else can happen. Our anxieties and worries recede, and in their place there can arise a profound *trust* in life, in destiny, in the forces within us. Many different things can cause anxiety and worry: what the day has in store; what the future holds; relationships with other people and much else. *Trust* in the face of all this lies in even deeper regions of the soul than peace, but they can also be reached. This trust is 'basically' also always there in us. It tells us that *everything* that happens — including painful experiences and crises, even those times when we fall short — is meaningful or can be placed meaningfully into the course of our destiny.

Talking about these even deeper experiences may at first seem very theoretical; however, the deeper the experience of peace becomes, the more apparent will they become. In fact such experiences make the experience of inner calm complete.

And we may strive to take a second step: out of tranquillity and trust we can come to feel *love* for the tasks that our destiny brings. We can learn to feel that there is *wisdom* in the demands of destiny, a wisdom whose ultimate aim, even in the face of life's difficulties, is to help us 'find ourselves.'

The three first steps:
- Tranquillity
- Trust in Destiny
- Love for my daily duties.

Constructive forces

> *Great thoughts and a pure heart — that is what we*
> *should ask from God in our prayers.*
> J.W. Goethe

We have now found a starting point for what is to live as spiritual content and prayer in the contemplative quiet of the soul; for quietness is only the 'vessel' for something else, for something essential.

We are not here concerned with the significance and practice of *meditation,* a subject which could also be pursued from the point we have arrived at. But before dealing specifically with *prayer,* let us turn for a moment to general human concerns, pertinent also for those who have no religious background. The following text may serve as an example:

Having established for yourself moments of inner peace, wrest yourself entirely free from your work-a-day life. Let your joys and sorrows, your cares and experiences, your actions pass in review before your soul; and let your attitude be such that you look at everything else in your experience from a higher standpoint ... at certain times you should seek the strength to stand towards yourself as towards a stranger, to confront your own self with the inner calmness of a judge. When you have learned to do this, your own experiences will show themselves to you in a new light ... During a calm inner survey the essential separates from the inessential. Sorrow and joy, every thought, every resolve wears a different guise when you confront yourself in this way.[*]

Another way of infusing the stillness of our soul with a content is to bring to life within ourselves for a moment a saying, a verse, a poem — perhaps something that is already familiar to us and which can serve to give our soul a positive orientation; or it may be something we choose specially to make the centre of our contemplation. There are any number of possibilities, and the most effective way will be for us to choose for ourselves what we are going to make the subject of our exercise.

Here are a few suggestions — just to get started!

Morning:
The light of the sun
Lights up the day
After dark of night;
The strength of the soul
It now awakes
From restful sleep:
O thou, my soul,
Give thanks to the light,
There shines forth in it
The power of God;
O thou my soul
Be strong for deeds.
        Rudolf Steiner

Evening:
I know from experience: neither the forces of death nor the forces of life, neither angels nor mights, neither things present nor things to come, not the World-Powers themselves, neither

---

[*] Rudolf Steiner, *Knowledge of the Higher Worlds.*

heights nor depths nor any other thing or Being in creation can separate us from the love of God which took on body in Christ Jesus, our Lord.

St Paul (Rom.8:38. Tr. J. Madsen)

Living in the word

We have already achieved a great deal when we have established the inner tranquillity we have been discussing; now we can simply speak our chosen words — out loud or in an undertone — perhaps several times; in between, we can make short pauses into which the stillness that we have already achieved can continue to flow. The more significant and profound our chosen words are, the more lasting and tangible will be the power emanating from them. We will find that words can have an intrinsic, radiating vitality that goes well beyond their being mere 'information'; and we can draw near to this radiating power in the way indicated.

We can do even more if we not only speak the text to ourselves but also try to make particular words come alive as much as possible. Take, for example, the words 'the light of the sun'; now call to mind for a moment the vast, streaming fullness of the sunlight — which is what the words describe, but which we by no means always feel when we read the words. For a moment we can live in the inner contemplation of the light. Similarly, with the words 'strength of soul': here we can dwell for a moment on the abundance and variety of the forces of the human soul. In such a manner we can bring to life the important content of a text and thereby make our inner awareness more real and strong.

Initially, this exercise leads into *contemplative meditation.* It can then revert to the *spoken word* in the way we have just discussed — except that now this has become more alive and meaningful than it could have been before. By degrees, we become able truly to 'live in the word.'

19

Praying is no longer a matter of course

Let us now move on to our main theme: Prayer. Many people feel no connection to prayer. Even those who, as children, were 'taught' to pray soon give up the habit after puberty, because they no longer see any sense in praying. They no longer have the sense that anything is really happening when they pray, and cannot conceive that anybody hears their prayers.

All this is very understandable in view of the fact that, since the beginning of the twentieth century, our religious ideas have been in a profound crisis. The fundamentals of religious life are being questioned on all sides. The *disadvantage* of this is that everything that, up to now, has been regarded as a matter of course is being shaken; but it also has the *advantage* that we now can work on these fundamentals in freedom and build them up out of our own insight.

To this end, the books by William Barclay may be found helpful; they represent a scholarly, but popular approach. *Prayer* by Olive Wyon deals with the subject from a more devotional angle. Parents with a young family will find Sarah Johnson's *Daring to be Different* a lively read.*

Beyond conventional theology, we can find in Rudolf Steiner's Anthroposophy an approach to an understanding of a spiritual world working with and above human beings, and the way to a new understanding of God.† In The Christian Community, moreover, there is a rich literature that can also act as a guide into the depths of Christianity in a new way, without ignoring the modern person's need for personal insight. Although they form the basis for

---

* William Barclay, *The Plain Man looks at the Lord's Prayer* (Collins) and *The Master's Men* (Collins). Olive Wyon, *Prayer* (Fontana). Sarah Johnson, *Daring to be Different* (Darton, Longman & Todd).

† For instance, Rudolf Steiner, *Religion: an Introductory Reader,* compiled by Andrew Welburn (Rudolf Steiner Press).

prayer, this is not the place to discuss all the fundamental questions concerning religion.

> *The soul can never be plumbed or mapped, for it is all-embracing.*
> Heraclitus

Prayer is a *personal turning to God.* In that sense, prayer goes a definite step beyond what has been discussed so far. But our minds are directed towards the creative power of the divine when we begin to live with the conviction that the picture of the world as a collection of meaningless, purely materialistic facts, structures and processes is not complete; rather, we realize that in the magnificent beauty of nature, in the form of the human body, the product of deepest wisdom, or in the great creations of the human spirit — to name just a few examples — much more comes to expression than mere material existence.

The advice and the suggestions given here are intended to help bring alive the image of the Godhead, to make it believable and accessible to our insight, even to our critical, present-day consciousness; to help us realize that God is not only the origin and foundation of the world, but is also our foundation and the fount of our being, as we are a part of this world.

> *A wise man said, 'Who would seek everywhere in the world around him for a tool he needed, when he knows it to be at home? It would be foolish. He, too, is a fool who seeks the instrument for the knowledge of God in the outer world when it lies at home within his soul.' Notice: he uses the words 'tool' and 'instrument.' It is not God we seek in the soul. He is sought by an instrument that is not found in the outer world, but in the soul, in prayer and genuine mystical absorption.*
> Rudolf Steiner

Origin and foundation of our life

Prayer is so significant and important for us because every day anew it can lead us towards the origin and sustaining foundation of our life. The conviction that there is a God and that we are involved with him may slowly take shape in us — but it will only become *real and effective* when we turn personally to God, in prayer. In praying we *activate* this conviction, we enter the sphere of our inner self that brings home to us the reality of the Godhead and thus re-affirms our conviction of God's existence. In this way we meet in prayer the fount of our actual life, the essence of our being.

The true nature of us human beings can only to a limited extent be deduced from our physical, 'natural' characteristics. Certainly, through our physical, material body, we are a part of earthly, material existence — it permeates us 'from below,' as it were. The same applies to our instincts and desires, many of which we have in common with the animals.

But 'from above' the essentially *human* aspect of the human being is also present in us, living in ideals and spiritual aims. Its chief characteristic is to be responsible, to have a conscience, to be *humane*, to be capable of feeling selfless love. This essence of our humanity senses and feels that life must have a purpose. None of these human capacities derive from nature — but then where do they come from? From 'above,' from the being of the Godhead who — as the Bible puts it — created the human being 'in his own image,' out of the forces of his inner being.

The great creations of the human spirit, the great works of art — of music, poetry, painting, sculpture and architecture, but also the genius of an actor or a gifted dancer, to name just a few, all of these demonstrate the 'higher' forces that are present in every human being. They can be seen as well in the great and small deeds of the human heart, the selfless love and willingness to help born out of true brotherliness and self-sacrifice. These higher powers shine out from the eyes of a little child; sometimes they become visible in the eyes of a dying person; they may become visible in many other moments throughout life. They live in the comforting hand of a mother, in the gesture of love between husband and wife, in the caring service of those who try to alleviate the sufferings of the sick. They are also at work in the longing of our hearts for greater humanity among human beings, for true peace on earth, for healing of the world.

In the book, *Knowledge of Higher Worlds,* Rudolf Steiner writes: 'In addition to what we may call their "everyday" persona, all human beings carry within them a higher being. This higher being remains hidden until it is awakened. And only we ourselves can awaken this higher human being in us.'

We have now touched on something of the 'higher' in us — that which does not originate from below but from above. It is with this part of our nature that we turn in prayer to the origin and foundation of our higher being. Here we see the deep tragedy of many modern human beings, whose path to prayer seems to be blocked. For they are cut off from the sphere of their own origin, and they are in danger of losing the foundation of their own existence. They lack a secure anchor for their being, so every crisis threatens to upset their inner equilibrium completely and make them insecure, even to drive them to despair. Often it is then late — though surely never too late — to search for the kind of inner support we have been discussing, and to seek refuge in prayer.

Stressful and traumatic situations often cause us to turn to the ultimate questions. If we understand 'ultimate' to mean 'last,' and leave them until last, they come too short; they should perhaps even be among our 'first' concerns. Surely the answer to the question, 'Where is the true origin of my whole being?' will determine my entire attitude to life. So long as I am in need or in danger, my turning to God will inevitably have a touch of egoism about it — if, indeed, I am able to establish the inner connection at all in such circumstances. Neither external nor internal need ought to drive us to prayer; rather, it is a question of having the free insight that in love and reverence we do really approach the highest in the world, that it is granted us to unite with God and allow his power to work in us.

Egoism in Prayer

One of the things that make many people shy away from prayer nowadays is that they find it impossible to attach any sensible meaning to religious concepts; another reason can often be the healthy feeling that prayer runs a real risk of becoming egotistic. While it is true that we are more likely to turn to prayer in a dangerous or traumatic situation, it is also then that the risk of egoism raises its head. Every personal prayer of intercession is subject to this danger; that is, every prayer in which we ask for this or that to *come about.*

> *Thou who art over us,*
> *Thou who art one of us,*
> *Thou who art -*
> *Also within us,*
> *May all see Thee — in me also,*
> *May I prepare the way for Thee,*
> *May I thank Thee for all that shall fall to my lot,*
> *May I also not forget the needs of others,*
> *Keep me in Thy love*
> *As Thou wouldest that all should be kept in mine.*
> *May everything in this my being be directed to Thy glory*
> *And may I never despair.*
> *For I am under Thy hand,*
> *And in Thee is all power and goodness.*
> *Give me a pure heart — that I may see Thee,*
> *A humble heart — that I may hear Thee,*
> *A heart of love — that I may serve Thee,*
> *A heart of faith — that I may abide in Thee.*
> Dag Hammarskjöld, (1905-61)

- In this connection, it is wonderful to realize that in the Lord's Prayer — the most profound prayer we have, originating with Christ himself — the personal 'requests' are *preceded* by 'thy will be done' — thus pre-empting all egoism: not what *I,* out of my limited insight, wish for is what should happen; but rather, that which would act on my life out of a higher insight, a higher will. With that, the danger of egoism is removed — provided, of course, that in speaking these words I seek to give them their full significance and weight.

- The fact that one can never truly say the Lord's Prayer for one-self only, but must include at least *one* other person, also works against egoism: I don't say 'my' but 'our,' not 'me' but 'us' etc. In saying 'our,' I am part of a community; this leads me beyond the limitations of my own self.

- On the other hand, this can often be a particular help for some-one starting on their life of prayer; many people find it easier to pray for *someone else* than for themselves. If we can feel con-vinced that true prayer accesses forces that can have a beneficial effect upon the destiny of another person close to us, then we are more likely to feel an impulse to pray than if we were doing it *only* for ourselves.

Intercession

Yet does not the danger of egoism, and, even more, of *subjectivity,* lurk just here? How, in interceding for others, can one know what is best for them?

Here the right underlying attitude for the intercession should surely also be: 'Thy will be done.' During the First World War, Rudolf Steiner formulated an intercessory prayer for the soldiers at the front. It was addressed to the 'genius,' the guardian angel of the human being — here called the 'active guardian spirit of your soul'

— who is asked to accept the love of the intercessor and convey it to the human being in question as fortifying strength for his destiny:

Spirit ever watchful,
Active guardian of your soul!
May your pinions carry
Our souls' petitioning love
To the one committed to your care upon earth;
That, united with your power,
Our prayer may radiate help
To the soul whom our love is seeking.

Here the prayer is not about something the intercessor wants to 'achieve' not even for one or more other persons (the prayer can be used in the plural too). Rather, the one who is praying calls up his 'petitioning love' and passes it on to the angel of the other person, in order that *he* may transform it into helping, fortifying strength, in accordance with what is important for the destiny of the other human being.

This inner attitude is exemplary: it avoids egoism and subjectivity in prayer.

• We simply cannot know, for instance, whether a serious illness is not, perhaps, precisely what is needed in the course of the other person's destiny, through which he or she may learn and achieve much of importance. It could therefore be quite wrong to pray for a rapid recovery. But we can pray that the ill or distressed person may be given strength to endure and gain the maturity intended by his or her destiny; we can help to cause *additional* love and help to flow into the ill or distressed person's situation to bring, if not *physical* relief, then *spiritual* strengthening and comfort.

• This approach is also right and appropriate for our own situation. We should not pray for our own (egoistic) wishes to be fulfilled, but that our inner relationship to the Godhead be strengthened. And incidentally, should we not actually welcome the hardships and trials sent by our destiny and which we need, perhaps to avoid becoming too soft and indolent and neglectful of the forces that we have been given?

• So in an intercessory prayer — but also in the speaking or praying of the Lord's Prayer with its 'Thy will be done,' there can be something that can take us beyond egoism in prayer. When we achieve this, our prayer *becomes* what it actually is and should be: a turning to God in love and freedom, a meeting with the foundation and origin of our being, a conversation with him who sustains us and who accepts into his love our incomplete being, complementing and fulfilling it.

The Lord's Prayer

The beginning

If we are coming new to prayer, or even if we are simply intending to refresh our life of prayer — we may be wondering about suitable texts. Of course, out of the inner peace we are striving to achieve we may to turn to God in silent worship and reverence, and it is also possible to express our present concerns quite freely in words arising spontaneously out of how we are feeling at that moment.

> *If a prayer did not owe its existence to the wisdom of worlds, it could not possess the warmth and light for the soul that we experience in true, profound prayer.*
> Rudolf Steiner

But there are also prayers born of a deeper insight, which are more than a collection of words chosen at random; they are, rather, something like a concentration of spiritual forces, of spiritual energy condensed into words. The prayer in which this process culminates is the Lord's Prayer. It was given by Christ himself. The disciples — so the gospel tells us — had felt the special power of his praying. They asked him to teach them to pray (Luke 11:1). He gave them the Lord's Prayer. Let us, for a moment, look at his choice of words, without going into too much detail.

As we have noted, even just the words of the Lord's Prayer, spoken sincerely, have the power to work against egoism in prayer: you can never speak this prayer for yourself only.

Something of the same is built into the structure, into the very sequence of sentences. It does not begin with the human concerns so close to our heart, but rather — underlining the fundamental gesture of every true prayer — with our turning to the Godhead. Not *our* affairs are put into the foreground; first we seek the relationship to God:

Our Father, who art in the heavens.

- At the beginning of this prayer, we can try to envisage the 'Father,' to imagine him as he is, in his all-encompassing being, his divine omnipotence, but also his fatherly closeness to us. We *enter into* this closeness, so that the word 'heavens' does not mean an unattainable beyond; rather, it comes to mean divine omnipresence — no place on earth is without its heaven — and at the same time it turns our soul to what is greater and more exalted than anything earthly.

- The Lord's Prayer begins, then, by 'raising' the soul. This in itself can be a kind of healing: for a moment we are freed from narrowness and small-mindedness; we are set free from the pressures of everyday life and can look up — and in looking up we become aware that something exists that is far greater and higher than everything which keeps us confined within our personal limitations. At that moment we may also begin to sense how we ourselves *belong* to this greater, higher, eternal Being; it is not alien to us — the relationship to the eternally Divine is so intimate that we are permitted to call it 'Father.'

- Obviously, many people in our age may find it difficult to feel any of this; various inner obstacles present themselves that are only too understandable nowadays. Perhaps we may not find it possible to use the Lord's Prayer straight away. Then we might use other texts to begin with, and perhaps we can approach the

Lord's Prayer gradually by immersing ourselves in more general religious questions, as discussed earlier.

- On the other hand, it is also possible to jump in at the deep end, trusting in the words of our chosen prayer. Gradually we may sense how, through its inherent form and composition, it becomes a creative power in the soul, *shaping* it so that the obstacles become unimportant; this is due to our ripening experience in connection with this prayer. Just as we can only learn to swim if we make up our mind to entrust ourselves to the water, and all the exercises that we can do on dry land don't really prepare us, so we can only learn to pray by praying.

A *classic example*

Simone Weil (1909–43), the French socialist, philosopher and mystic, was born in Paris into an agnostic Jewish family and was brought up in a humanist environment. Her father, Bernard Weil, was a doctor and her mother came from a wealthy family of businessmen.

In the mid-1930s, Weil became increasingly drawn to Christianity, and in 1937 at the chapel of St Francis in Assisi, Italy, she had one of her mystical experiences.

In Solesmes, France, she met a young Englishman who gave her the poem 'Love' by George Herbert. She learnt it by heart in order to have instant access to it whenever she had one of her blinding, debilitating headaches. 'I thought I was just reciting a beautiful poem, but speaking this poem had, unknown to me, the power of a prayer. Once, while I was speaking it ... Christ himself came down and touched me. Through the suffering I felt the presence of love like the one you see in the smile of a beloved face ...'

From her own experience, she was now aware of the existence of a divine world, and from a Christian friend she got to know the Lord's Prayer in Greek. Enchanted by the beauty of the language, and also because of a promise she had made, she learned it by heart and, during the grape harvest, spoke it every morning and occasionally also while working.

'Since that time, as my only exercise, I have undertaken to speak it every morning with total concentration. If my attention wanders or weakens while I am speaking, I begin again until I have completed it once with my entire attention. Sometimes I then start from the beginning once more for the sheer joy of it, but only if I have a strong urge to do so. The power of this exercise is extraordinary and surprises me every time, and although I experience it every day, it always surpasses my expectations ... on occasion, while I am praying or at other moments, Christ is present in person, but his presence is infinitely more real, more clear and loving than it was when he first came to me.'

Simone Weil died at the age of 34 of tuberculosis in Ashford, England, in 1943. She refused food and medical treatment out of sympathy for the plight of the people of Occupied France.

T.S. Eliot called her 'a woman of genius, of a kind of genius akin to that of the saints.' Her experience seems particularly pertinent to our subject here, since it did *not* arise out of a religious tradition but was something that happened in a quite natural, immediate way to a wide-awake, self-aware human being of our time; and furthermore, it was not a once-only happening but an ongoing, recurring event.

> *Love bade me welcome; yet my soul drew back,*
>   *Guilty of dust and sin.*
> *But quick-ey'd Love, observing me grow slack*
>   *From my first entrance in,*
> *Drew nearer to me, sweetly questioning*
>   *If I lack'd any thing.*

> 'A guest,' I answer'd, 'worthy to be here.'
>   Love said, 'you shall be he.'
> 'I the unkind, ungrateful? Ah my dear,
>   I cannot look on thee.'
> Love took my hand, and smiling did reply,
>   'Who made the eyes but I?'
>
> 'Truth, Lord, but I have marr'd them; let my shame
>   Go where it doth deserve.'
> 'And know you not,' says Love, 'who bore the blame?'
>   'My dear, then I will serve.'
> 'you must sit down,' says Love, 'and taste my meat.'
>   So I did sit and eat.
> George Herbert (1593–1633)

The Lord's Prayer, continuation

Let us continue our contemplation of the Lord's Prayer. We have already noted that the first step is for the soul to 'rise up' and turn to the 'Father in the heavens.' When we manage this, we have already begun to free ourselves from the 'weight' of our earthly existence; and that, at the same time, means that we are also beginning to 'remember' our own eternal nature and to 'touch in' to it.

The next three sentences are also wholly orientated towards the being of God:

> *Hallowed be* thy *name.*
> Thy *kingdom come,*
> Thy *will be done,*
> *as above in the heavens so also on the earth.*

Notice that in the Lord's Prayer we are at first repeatedly deflected from our human circumstances, in order that we can turn all the more unhindered to the experience of the divine. In prayer, we are not seeking enhancement of our own *earthly,* egoistic personality, nor the glorification of *our* name: we can feel here the antidote to the problem of excessive ambition and thirst for glory. We are not seeking to enlarge *our* sphere of influence — the antidote to the desire to dominate — and we are not asking that *our* will should prevail. With the first sentences of the Lord's Prayer we learn to sense that, far from losing ourselves by turning towards God and freeing ourselves from our own merely personal wishes, we actually only find and strengthen our best forces when we free them from the stranglehold of egoism. Only when we enter into the sphere of the *eternal* does the *temporal* side of our life come into its rightful proportions. It is not that it is rejected or pushed aside; it is just put in its proper place. We will find that this inner 'adjustment' through the first sentences already has an extraordinary healing aspect. It acts as a counterbalance to much that we do — and often are obliged to do — elsewhere in life. It enables us to place something on the other side of the scales of our life, so as to restore the *equilibrium* that we have already spoken about.

But then, with the following sentences, our earthly destiny is also integrated fully:

> *Give* us *this day our daily bread.*
> *And forgive* us *our trespasses,*
> *As we forgive those who trespass against* us.
> *And lead* us *not into temptation,*
> *But deliver* us *from the evil.*

Each sentence addresses fundamental questions of earthly existence and relates them to the working of the divine, 'raises' them onto a higher plane. The daily *bread* means more than merely physical nourishment; it embraces everything that can nourish inwardly — as in the saying: 'man does not live by bread alone.' The *trespasses* (or *debts*) are unavoidable, not only where we fail actively, but also where we remain indebted to ourselves or to others. And finally there is *evil,* the terrible threat that confronts us in our earthly existence. When we pray these words, we offer up to God everything that entangles us in worries and anxiety, so that in the struggle for daily bread (and likewise when enjoying worldly goods) we do not get enslaved by the world. Then we are not destroyed by guilt but may hope for forgiveness and recompense through him whose will is at work in all human destiny; so that we shall not be dragged into the abyss by evil.

The sentence about 'temptation' can cause some problems. It is not easy to experience or understand how it is possible that God could lead us into temptation. Much thought has gone into trying to understand this request. The following interpretation seems particularly persuasive: precisely in the turning to God are we exposed to temptations, such as, for instance, to practise religious devotion in a one-sided way. We are then in danger of neglecting practical life, our daily duties and earthly tasks. Excessive wallowing in religious emotions or religious fanaticism and dogmatic self-righteousness are often the consequences of a one-sided religious life. So this prayer is that our dedication to the divine shall not lead to the kind of one-sidedness that *can* be caused by the powerful attraction that God exerts upon the soul.

> *In seeking to escape from the world, we can become false angels, proud and loveless; or we can become worse than animals in ignominious enslavement to the world. We need to strengthen the power of the centre, of mediation — the essentially human element.*
> Rudolf Frieling

In the first part of the Lord's Prayer we turned to God with all the devotion of which we are capable; we 'tuned in' to the eternal. Now, in turn, we can feel in the second part that we are not left alone by God in our earthly cares and dangers.

In conclusion, the Lord's Prayer again turns to God:

> *For Thine is the kingdom*
> *the power*
> *and the glory*
> *for ever and ever.*

Although this ending does not come from Christ himself — it was added to the Lord's Prayer in the first centuries as the community's response to the prayer — it is surely rightly held to be a worthy close to the preceding text.

Is our prayer heard?

It can be difficult to imagine that anyone actually *listens* to our prayer, let alone that there is someone who *hears* it.

Perhaps the following personal experience may be helpful. In the period immediately after the war, when I was a schoolboy of fourteen or fifteen, it was especially important to work hard at school to catch up, owing to the fact that much school work had been neglected. Often, a written exam could decide one's career prospects. I remember that on one occasion I asked the good Lord expressly for the success of a piece of work: I prayed for good marks. The outcome was negative. That made a deep impression on me — after all, I really had made an inner effort, and now was it all for nothing?

I know that disappointments of this kind — although admittedly usually in connection with more serious, crucial questions — can mean the end of all trust in God. If God does not hear me when I earnestly ask him for something, why should I still concern myself with him? Perhaps he does not even exist! Who could say that such questions are not justified?

It dawned upon me at the time that something was not right. Was it necessarily God's fault? Was it really a reason to doubt His existence? Or was there something wrong with my prayer?

This personal example shows clearly that my approach was wrong from the very beginning. One should not trouble the good Lord with something one can and should do by one's own effort. The old saying, 'God helps those who help themselves,' is absolutely right. My prayer ought not to have taken the place of my own efforts; but it could have given me peace, confidence and strength in the knowledge that my destiny was in the hands of a higher power.

Here is the deciding factor which we have already discussed in connection with egoism in prayer. Of course it is easy to understand when someone wrestles in prayer for the life of a beloved human being who is in mortal danger, or when a person prays for his own deliverance from peril. This is all perfectly natural. And yet: 'thy will be done' smoothes the path to a profound trust in one's destiny. Perhaps it cannot always be spoken with *ease,* especially when we have just *begun* to pray. Still, a more profound trust in destiny can be the fruit of a longer experience of praying. It is precisely in the crucial moments of life, when our trust in the wisdom and love of the divine guidance of our destiny is challenged most radically that we will experience the power of prayer. We will be able to say, 'my prayer has been "heard".'

The aim of our praying, then, should not be that this or that wish be granted on the strength of our prayer; rather, it should be that we may find strength, trust and love of our earthly destiny. And for that the Lord's Prayer is the very best guide; furthermore it is the source of 'spiritual energies' in the form of thoughts and words which can equip us inwardly with the strength we need on our inner path. We have just seen something of this kind in the case of Simone Weil. It has also been the experience throughout the centuries of all who pray.

Even if we are able to accept this way of looking at things, there still remains the question: 'is there really somebody who *hears* me when I pray? Can I seriously believe that my speaking reaches the consciousness, the "ear" of God? Is this not a ridiculous assumption to make?'

The question will now be whether we can slowly develop our concepts so that they can approach the reality of God. Certainly, initially this reality lies outside or above what one can grasp with one's normal powers of imagining. After all, our conceptions are formed by the limited *earthly* reality. If we try and call up before our inner perception the eternal, infinite nature of God, this in itself is a crossing of boundaries. And yet we can begin by trying to embrace the thought that for the Godhead the constrictions and limitations of earthly existence do not apply, neither as regards his consciousness, nor in relation to the fullness and omnipresence of his being. In fact, this is the *essence* of divine reality: that it encompasses everything and permeates everything — it is this that makes it a *divine* being.

Even among *human beings* there are various levels of consciousness: beginning with the person who only ever thinks about him or herself; then the mother who holds in her consciousness a family, who knows 'instinctively' when one of them is not well; and there is the teacher who embraces a whole class with his or her consciousness and feelings. When we contemplate *God,* we must imagine this step-by-step widening of the human consciousness multiplied to infinity. He embraces and bears all the beings who have come forth from Him. He is 'close' to them all.

> *Once, he was absorbed in prayer in a quiet place. And when he paused, one of his disciples said to him, 'Lord, teach us the way of prayer, as John also taught it to his disciples.' And he said to them, 'When you pray, say this ...' [There follows the Lord's Prayer]*
> Luke 11:1f. Tr. Jon Madsen

Let us remind ourselves that the Lord's Prayer was given by Christ himself. It was he who taught the disciples to speak: 'Our Father ...' He would have been misleading his disciples if there were no-one there to hear and respond with his being to these words. But the disciples had just sensed in Christ the power of his prayer, springing from his one-ness with the Father. In the light of this experience they would have known: God hears every sincere prayer.

The actual 'hearing' of our prayer is this: with all our cares, indeed with our whole existence, we may feel raised up into the being of God; for a moment we may feel sheltered, and this fills our whole being with solace, strength and courage.

Peace, trust, love, thankfulness

At this point let us return to some of the motifs we have already considered. We spoke of peace as the starting point for any spiritual endeavour, and that it is good if prayer can also flow from the inner peace which we discussed earlier. First we can try to enter into this inner stillness as well as we are able at that particular moment, and to become engulfed by it. Arising out of this stillness, this inner peace, our prayer can reach greater depths, too.

A next step can be to stop after each sentence and 'return' to the stillness before going on to the next sentence. We should, of course, feel free to do what seems most appropriate for us. Sometimes it will be enough to stay with one sentence or just one word for a while. We can also deepen our experience of the Lord's Prayer by repeating it one or more times until we are entirely 'within' it. We saw how, in the case of Simone Weil, this repeated speaking of the prayer was a decisive help. Through experiment we will gradually discover what is best for us, and can then check from time to time to see if there is anything that needs to be done differently.

As we have already seen, inner peace can grow into *trust,* trust in destiny. This becomes more tangible in connection with prayer. We have called trust the 'fruit' of prayer. Here, inner peace *leading* to prayer and the trust engendered when this peace is *enhanced* by prayer, enrich one another mutually.

We can find this effect of prayer especially important in the morning, when the events of the coming day may be causing us worry and anxiety. We may not always succeed, at any rate not to begin with, but in time we will certainly find that even in difficult moments in our life, trust in our destiny — 'Thy will be done' — can arise from peace-filled prayer, from praying peacefulness.

And as a consequence of this prayerful peace and trust we will be able to take a further step. We will learn to *love* our tasks and duties on earth. Already by learning to feel trust in our destiny we are becoming aware that we are not the plaything of blind, meaningless chance. Rather, we are being guided by a purpose-filled destiny, and ultimately everything that happens will be what is good and right. It is not only possible to trust such a destiny — we can feel love for it! And this destiny then also includes the tasks and daily duties which may sometimes be irksome but which we can come to think of as also belonging to the wise guidance of our destiny. In this way trust in destiny deepens into love, love for the tasks that the day brings.

For when we say 'thy will be done,' it is not, of course, meant to be only with the feeling of having to bow to the inevitable, of having to put up with what is anyhow unavoidable. Especially at the beginning of a new day, we will slowly be able to find the right mood of love for everyday life when we enter into prayer in the right way. In this way praying becomes a path that can give strength for our destiny, strength that has the power to heal the weakness of the human soul.

I shall know why, when time is over,
And I have ceased to wonder why;
Christ will explain each separate anguish
In the fair schoolroom of the sky.

He will tell me what Peter promised,
And I, for wonder at his woe,
I shall forget the drop of anguish
That scalds me now, that scalds me now.
Emily Dickinson (1830-86)

So far we have looked particularly at the 'mood of prayer in the morning' and how linked it is to *trust*. But of course the evening also has its special mood of prayer; in fact, we may even find it easier to come to rest, inwardly, then. The problems of everyday life have fallen away to some extent, though the experiences of the past hours still reverberate in the soul. Now try to become calm. On looking back, our mood can be one of thankfulness, out of which we then speak the prayer: thankfulness that our life has been preserved, that we have had nourishment for body and soul; indeed thankfulness for everything good and beautiful that we received as nourishment for our soul in the course of the day. And lastly, thankfulness that the wrongs we have committed and the debts we have incurred can be raised into the divine forgiveness and reparation, and that we were saved from falling prey to evil. In this way, the first part of the Lord's Prayer is particularly meaningful for the beginning of the day, the second part for the evening.

Using the Lord's Prayer as an example, we have now explored some fundamental elements that can lead to a deepening of prayer. But at this point let it be said quite clearly that we may also want to leave all this on one side. We should not be under the impression that in order to pray properly it is absolutely essential that we call up in our soul the moods and feelings we have been indicating. These were only suggestions which may be helpful. Anyone who can pray without such aids will do so, quite rightly. And above all: if we cannot always find the time to develop the preparatory mood and stillness, let us just speak the words of the prayer. Certainly, it is better to pray as well as is possible at the given moment, than not to pray at all for lack of time. If need be, even *one* word, *one* thought will serve to connect us to the reality of prayer; and this means that we avoid letting the moment that we otherwise set aside for prayer go by, unused. The same applies in cases of serious illness or extreme weakness or exhaustion when it can happen that there is not even strength enough for praying.

The Healing Power of Prayer

The main subject of this little book has been touched on repeatedly. We began with the observation that more and more people are becoming ill and unbalanced from causes arising in the soul and spirit. This raised the question of what help there might be in this situation. We spoke, in quite general terms, about the restoration of the balance to much of the one-sidedness of contemporary life, about the creation of inner stillness, about filling this stillness with meaningful content. We then also looked at the strength that can flow from the first regular practice of prayer.

> *Poor soul, the centre of my sinful earth,*
> *Fooled by these rebel powers that thee array,*
> *Why dost thou pine within and suffer dearth,*
> *Painting thy outward walls so costly gay?*
> *Why so large cost, having so short a lease,*
> *Dost thou upon thy fading mansion spend?*
> *Shall worms, inheritors of this excess,*
> *Eat up thy charge? Is this thy body's end?*
> *Then, soul, live thou upon thy servant's loss,*
> *And let that pine to aggravate thy store;*
> *Buy terms divine in selling hours of dross;*
> *Within be fed, without be rich no more:*
> *So shalt thou feed on Death, that feeds on men,*
> *And Death once dead, there's no dying then.*
> William Shakespeare (Sonnet 146)

To find peace in the soul brings a healing influence to bear on the restlessness that otherwise fills us, and which will without fail eventually have an impact on our physical condition and may ultimately even cause us to fall ill. Even more profound is the effect when trust and love can arise in the soul, when we succeed for a few moments in pushing aside fear and worry, frustration and aggression, and instead immerse ourselves in positive forces within. The more successful we are in this, the more we may find that the tensions and deep-seated frustrations that we bear within us as part of modern life can be resolved.

And we can take a further step in praying: then not only calm, trust and love grow within us, but we rise above ourselves and encounter the higher, the eternal that has existed from the very beginning, which is also the fount and origin of our essential being. Then, as we have seen, not only do we free ourselves for a moment from the oppressiveness and constraints of our normal life and cast off the fetters of egoism, but in the encounter with the divine our soul receives profound, healing powers.

To clarify: 'healing' does not only mean 'restoring to health.' As with the word 'wholesome,' there can also be the sense of 'making whole' what has been damaged or injured. In that sense, then, 'healing' would mean restoring something which has lost its wholeness.

The essence of our being does not originate in the earthly world. As we saw earlier, our essential humanness derives from 'above' rather than from 'below.' But through living in the earthly sphere we lose contact with our own eternal origin. We let go of the 'anchor' that secures us to the being of God. In doing so, we have already lost our inner support, long before a blow of destiny can deprive us of it outwardly, too. We have lost our inner equilibrium long before we become aware of it, so that we may say: we have lost the wholeness of our being, we are no longer 'whole' — we need healing.

> *If you abide in me and my words live on in you, pray for that which you also will, and it shall come about for you. By this my Father is revealed, that you bear much fruit and become ever more my disciples.*
> John 15:7. Tr. Jon Madsen

It will surely be obvious that we are not here talking about something for which anybody can be blamed — a failing, or worse still, a moral defect. What we are talking about here is simply the fundamental condition of earthly life into which we are born and which we have to endure without, initially, being able to do anything to change it.

On the other hand, the real reason for any amount of frustration and discontent, for the vague longings and restless seeking of so many people — not least of many young people — is to be found in this 'unwholesome' basic state of our earthly existence. Cut off from the roots of our human existence, bereft of 'anchorage' in the eternal, we are bound to end up feeling insecure, subject to doubts and despair, fears and depression; we have lost our bearings and suffer from constant restlessness. It is easy to understand that this can also give rise to a whole range of bodily diseases; it is also probable that the susceptibility of many people to drugs and sensationalism of all kinds has its origins here.

Religion is actually nothing else but an attempt to restore our relationship with the world from which we have come. One of the explanations of the origins of the word 'religion' is to 'reconnect,' that is, to re-establish our link with the realms that we cannot do without in the long run if we are not to suffer harm. A prayer, divine service, a sacrament — these all return us to the reality that is our true home. This is why a genuine religious life is no 'superstructure,' no idealistic addition to the 'actual' reality of life; it is the basis, the foundation that enables us truly to stand in the earthly world.

One is bound to admit, though, that religious life, as it presents itself in various ways nowadays, has often lost its genuineness, its seriousness and depth. It may perhaps even be pervaded by sentimentality and subtle egoism; but let this not dissuade us from our own striving for religious experience that is genuine and earnest and that goes deep; and maybe we will feel moved to seek for others who are striving after this, too. We will then also discover that everywhere a stream of wholesome religious life continues to flow.

Sleeping and waking

Not for nothing have we been placing special emphasis on *prayer in the evening and in the morning.* Obviously, we can pray at any moment of the day; and yet the moments when we enter sleep and awake out of it are particularly suited for prayer.

For what is sleep, actually? It is the result of the soul freeing itself from the body; outwardly, we remain unconscious; it is only in dreams that we occasionally become dimly aware that this unconsciousness perhaps is not total after all, that even in sleep things are 'going on' in us. In an impressive way, Rudolf Steiner spoke about the nocturnal experiences of the soul — experiences that we leave behind again on waking and then often can only recall to consciousness as a soul-mood:

> For many people in our materialistic times it is very, very difficult to feel what I should like to call the holiness, the sacredness of sleep. It is an aberrant cultural phenomenon when the intelligence inherent in mankind has lost all respect for the sanctity of sleep. We must obviously live with the world, but we must live with the world with our eyes open, because only then can we wrest our bodily nature away from the 'lower' side of our nature in order to elevate it; just imagine how many people there are who spend their evening occupied with things of a purely materialistic kind and then pass into sleep without developing the feeling — it cannot really come to life out of a materialistic mentality — without developing the feeling: sleep unites us with the spiritual world, sleep sends us across to the spiritual world.
>
> It would be to their benefit if people would at least gradually become able to feel and say to themselves: "I am going to sleep. Until I wake up, my soul will be in the spiritual world. There it will meet my guardian angel. And when I wake up, I will have met this angel. The wings of my angel will have wafted around my soul."

As regards the overcoming of a materialistic life, it makes all the difference in the world whether or not one is able to call up this feeling when thinking of one's relationship to sleep.

One can only overcome this materialistic way of life by engendering intimate feelings, feelings of a kind that are also in accord with the spiritual world.

When we manage to make such feelings really alive within us, then our life in sleep will become so potent that, in turn, our contact with the spiritual world will increase until our waking life, too, can gradually be active enough for us to be surrounded not only by the world of the senses but also by the spiritual world which actually is the real world, the truly real world. For this world, the one that we usually call 'the real world' is, of course, only an image of the real world. The real world is the world of the spirit. [*]

If we can relate and 'warm' to such ideas, we will be able to develop still further the differentiation between prayer in the evening and in the morning. We will be able to say to ourselves, 'With my evening prayer I increase the power that leads me into these higher spheres. In praying I spread the wings that take me to my meeting with my "genius," the angel who accompanies my destiny. And in this very encounter with my angel I will be given the strength that I need in everyday life in the form of stillness, trust and love. At the same time, my encounter with the angel is also a living assurance that my relationship to the Godhead is not completely broken off even if, during the day, I have to be active in quite other realms of life. The angel "stands before God" and "anchors" my existence in the being of the divine.'

Rudolf Steiner's remarks about the holiness of sleep are even more pertinent now than when he first made them; but in connection with the word 'holiness' it is good to think mainly of its relationship

[*] *Cosmic and Human Metamorphosis*, lecture 3

to 'wholeness,' rather than to give undue weight to the sentimentality that sometimes clings to this word. We are again in the realm of *healing* — of the *making whole* of our human nature. It is very helpful to have this word used in connection with sleep.

Modern life also makes it difficult for the soul to 'ascend' in the night; the 'wings' of the soul no longer unfold, they do not bear us aloft if, during the day, we only live with earthly concerns and have no wish to give a thought to a higher world. But quiet contemplation in the evening, and prayer, provide the 'momentum' that empowers us to meet with the genius of our destiny.

> *O soft embalmer of the still midnight,*
> *Shutting with careful fingers and benign,*
> *Our gloom-pleas'd eyes, embowered from the light,*
> *Enshaded in forgetfulness divine:*
> *O soothest Sleep! If so it please thee, close*
> *In midst of this thine hymn my willing eyes,*
> *Or wait the 'Amen' ere thy poppy throws*
> *Around my bed its lulling charities.*
> *Then save me, or the passèd day will shine*
> *Upon my pillow, breeding many woes -*
> *Save me from curious conscience, that still lords*
> *Its strength for darkness, burrowing like a mole;*
> *Turn the key deftly in the oilèd wards,*
> *And seal the hushèd Casket of my soul.*
> J. Keats

And what of the morning? Here, too, we will find the transition — this time from sleep to wakefulness — very significant. For, depending on our inner attitude, the forces in which we have been immersed while asleep will either carry over into waking life or they will fade as we awaken. But there is actually something we will be able to do about this. The wings of the soul may be folded again, but they have something of the 'dew' of divine life about them. It is not only plants that are soaked and refreshed with dew in the morning. The soul, too, brings back refreshment and strength from the spiritual world. We can try to ensure that it is not immediately darkened by the 'dust' of earth, that it learns to hold on to the touch of the forces of its own origins.

Healing of the soul and healing of the body

So far we have not mentioned that praying also can lead to *bodily* healing — not always, but in certain circumstances. In some religious communities it is even made the central objective of their religious practice.

In our view, religious striving and feeling can all too easily become egoistic in this way, the very thing, surely, that must be avoided, as we have already mentioned. It does not seem fitting to turn to God preoccupied in this way with egoistic wishes.*

The effect of prayer, in the first instance, is that it can unfold healing powers in the soul. These have an impact on the vast field of soul-spiritual causes of those illnesses that we see encroaching upon us more and more; and these illnesses can ultimately also lead to bodily, physical disease. So we are dealing with *genuine powers of healing* when we open our soul to stillness, trust, love and, above all, to prayer. These powers bring healing to the sphere from which further causes of illness would otherwise flow into the body.

Whether or not these healing powers will also work directly upon our *physical* organism, that we must leave to destiny. (Whether or not healing can or should take place is, above all, a question of destiny; for the function of every healing is to stimulate and activate something in the human being.) There is no need to doubt such effects in principle, but to make it one's specific *intention* to bring them about would be to allow oneself to sink back into personal

* Even Christ himself did not always heal all the sick of his time; the gospel accounts show clearly that the right moment of destiny always played a role in these healings.

egoism, in the very act of praying which is supposed to raise us up to God. This would be the opposite of what one is striving for. It is *possible* that one might experience bodily recovery and relief, but the soul would suffer all the greater harm.

Now, fortunately, there is the art of the physician which, to a large extent, can provide treatment and healing. Even a very serious illness can often be warded off, or a critically ill person restored to life. But here the question can arise: what will the person do with the gift of a new life? He was close to death; now his life has been given back to him again. Will he go on living in the same way as before, or will he be able to understand his illness as a 'message' from destiny that something in his life has to change?

For doctors it is often dispiriting to observe how a person whom they have helped to regain his health and return to daily life will carry on wasting his life senselessly. It is not only falling ill that poses a challenge from our destiny, getting well again also calls upon us to ponder our future life, to bring order into it and shape it anew in accordance with the equilibrium of the soul. In this respect the various suggestions we have been making can be especially useful.

> *The inmost feelings that are stirred in prayer teach even the simplest of us something of the infinite expanses of soul life.*
> Rudolf Steiner

But although we might not make our wish to be healed of a bodily, physical illness the central concern of our praying, prayer can nevertheless be the most decisive support, not least at such very difficult times in life as when we are ill. Such prayer will not usually lead to physical, bodily healing, but strength, courage and comfort will grow in the soul, helping one to bear one's destiny; *patience* will prove to be the fruit of that kind of prayer.

Anyone who has much contact with the sick and the dying knows that the manner in which they come to terms with their suffering does not depend on the severity of their affliction. What decides whether they have the strength and patience to bear the inevitable, is entirely a matter of their soul's strength. When the soul has inner strength, even very severe suffering can be borne in a quite astonishing way. If the soul has no inner security, even a slight burden leads to a breakdown. That is why we are investigating ways to develop such inner strength and security of soul.

Constancy

We began this little book by looking at how difficult it can be nowadays to keep up the momentum of inner work. Frequently, the inner determination required flags sooner or later. To end with, let us return to this problem.

To counteract this waning resolve, we can begin by giving careful thought to our proposed 'programme.' As we have already said, we should not attempt too much all at once, not for too long, not straight away for the rest of our life, but, initially, only for a short period at a time.

On the other hand, of course, inner endeavours only unfold their full power if they are sustained for years and decades, not just for a few weeks or months. But precisely because one generally has to acquire the necessary staying power first, it is advisable to proceed purposefully, step by step.

Nevertheless, even if we do this — and this is true of all spiritual endeavours that are practised on a regular basis for any length of time — after a while we may come to feel that we are no longer quite 'in' what we are trying to do. Many people experience this also in connection with prayer. The words seem to become empty or formulaic, and it feels as though we can no longer live fully in them. However, this is no reason for giving up praying. Even then, rather than stop praying altogether, it is better just to speak the Lord's Prayer, for instance, as best we can at that moment. Just as we sometimes eat, even if we do not at that moment particularly feel like it, because we know that it is necessary if we are to keep up our strength and that our health will be affected if we do not, so also we can turn to prayer even if, temporarily, we don't derive any satisfaction from it. Whatever else, there is substance and strength in the words, as there is in food, even if on occasion we eat only because it is necessary.

> *The power of the true centre, resting in itself and capable of mediating between heaven and earth, is revealed in the human 'I.'*
> Rudolf Frieling

At the same time remedial intervention is obviously needed. One way could be that we make time, apart from the time set aside for prayer, to ponder single words or sentences of the prayer anew. There is a rich field of literature which may be helpful. We don't have to read all of the books from cover to cover; often it will be enough to contemplate one or two pages. Any new ideas can stimulate us to see in a new light what perhaps has become over-familiar, and so to re-enliven it that new strength begins to flow into the prayer itself. We may have to repeat this process occasionally, just as a plant has to be watered now and again to be given new forces of life.

The story of Simone Weil contains a hint that may be helpful whenever we fell ourselves flagging: the Lord's Prayer can increase in intensity when it is prayed with devotion several times in succession; the same can be done with single sentences.

Finally, let us call to mind something that can be the real key for gaining access to the realm of prayer. Every true prayer is also an intercession, which includes other people. This thought may be helpful when it comes to traversing the occasional 'desert' in our praying.

If we can practise constancy in this innermost sphere of our life, then we help to build the foundation of existence.

Human beings need inner constancy,
Faithful constancy towards the guidance of the
spiritual beings.
Upon this constancy they can build
Their eternal existence and essence
And thereby permeate and strengthen
The world of the senses
With eternal light.
Rudolf Steiner

Particular Forms of Prayer

For the dead

In conclusion, let us consider some particular forms of prayer. First, let us look at prayer for those who have died. It is especially important to think of them and to pray for them. This idea may seem strange at first. Some people cannot imagine that there might be conscious life beyond the threshold of death and that our thoughts can have any possible effect there; others believe that in 'heaven' all difficulties cease, and that the departed souls should be thought of as being in an 'exalted' state, separated from the sufferings of life.

Neither of these ideas corresponds to the facts. In a short book such as this, it is obviously not possible to give detailed reasons for this statement. In the New Testament, there is what might called a 'glimpse into the afterlife' in the story told by Jesus of the rich man and Lazarus. This makes it very clear that the soul's experiences after death are vivid and of great significance:

Once there was a rich man, dressed in purple and fine linen. Every day he held splendid and merry feasts. And a poor man named Lazarus lay in front of his entrance hall, covered with sores, and begged for the scraps from the rich man's table to still his hunger. And the dogs came and licked his sores. Now the poor man died and was carried by angels to Abraham's bosom. And the rich man also died and was buried. And in the realm of shadows, where he had to endure great suffering, he lifted up his eyes and saw Abraham from afar, and he saw Lazarus in his bosom. And he called out: 'Father Abraham, have mercy on me and send Lazarus to dip his fingertip in water and cool my tongue with it, for I am suffering in this flame!' But Abraham said, 'My son, remember that you had goods in your earthly life; but Lazarus only had what was bad. Now he is receiving comfort for his soul here, and you are suffering. And what is more, a great chasm separates us from you; no one wanting to cross from here to you is able to do so, nor can anyone pass from there to us.' Then he said, 'Then I beg you, father, to send him to the house of my father, for I have five brothers. I want him to be a witness to the truth for them, so that they do not also come to this place of torment.' But Abraham said, 'They have Moses and the prophets; let them hear them.' He replied, 'No, father Abraham, if someone rises from the dead and comes to them, then they will change their hearts and minds.' But he said, 'If they do not heed Moses and the prophets, neither will they heed one who rises from the dead.'

Luke 16,19–31. Tr. Jon Madsen

Not for nothing, then, has it always been Christian practice to pray for the dead. Their consciousness extends beyond the threshold of death and it is by no means the case that the *inner* bonds that tie them to their earthly destiny are severed immediately when the *outward* bonds are loosened by death. In particular, truly significant human relationships do not simply cease to exist after death — on the contrary: since everything physical has now fallen away, the needs of the soul and spirit emerge all the more urgently, with almost elemental force.These needs are, above all, the desire for human fellowship, for that inner warmth and the spiritual light that can live in loving human caring attentiveness.

In this respect countless departed human souls today suffer painful deprivation; they feel as though cast out from the human community because their nearest and dearest whom they left behind have almost forgotten them. In the cold loneliness of their after-death existence, each loving thought sent to them by us is then like a ray of light and warmth; and each heartfelt prayer creates something like a veritable life-giving centre, an oasis in the 'desert' of misery that otherwise surrounds the human soul in its experiences of death.

From this viewpoint we can see the importance of praying for the departed if we are able to pray. We could, of course, combine this with the Lord's Prayer by thinking of the departed as vividly as possible and include them in the word 'our.' There are, however, also other prayers. I have found the following, given by Rudolf Steiner, especially suitable.

> My love be woven as an offering
> into the sheaths which now surround you,
> cooling all heat,
> warming all coldness.
> Do thou live upwards
> borne by love,
> endowed with light!

For the sick

In a seriously ill person the soul's activity often wanes; maybe the patient can just about manage to think or speak a few words of a prayer, but it will prove a great blessing if now there is someone who not only provides loving care, but who also prays with and for him. Here, too, we should bear in mind that if the relatives of a sick person neglect this, they are failing to do what is perhaps most important of all.

Obviously, it is essential that the patient also wants this. On enquiring, we may be surprised to find that a person who otherwise has not had any religious feelings — or at least has never shown any — suddenly, on coming into contact with deeper levels of their soul in this situation, can feel that it is right and necessary to do something of this kind. Simone Weil's biography points in this direction. Perhaps, if we summon up the courage to ask, we may be able to help someone find the way back to prayer.

Again, the Lord's Prayer can be used. But we can also select texts that are familiar to the patient or which are remembered from childhood. Psalm 23 is particularly suitable.

> The Lord is my shepherd,
> I shall not want.
> He makes me lie down in green pastures,
> He leads me beside still waters
> He restores my soul.
> He leads me in right paths for His name's sake.
> Even though I walk through the valley of the shadow
> of death
> I fear no evil,
> For Thou art with me,
> Thy rod and Thy staff they comfort me.
> Thou preparest a table before me in the presence of
> my enemies,
> Thou anointest my head with oil,
> my cup overflows.
> Surely goodness and mercy shall follow me
> All the days of my life
> And I shall dwell in the house of the Lord for ever.

There is also the following verse for the sick by Rudolf Steiner:

> O Spirit of God permeate me
> Permeate me in my soul;
> My soul endow with strong power,
> Strong power give also to my heart,
> My heart that seeks Thee
> Seeks Thee through deep longing,

Deep longing for healing life,
For healing life and courage,
Courage that into my limbs does stream,
Does stream as a noble gift divine,
Gift divine from Thee, O Spirit of God,
O Spirit of God permeate me.

For children

It is the particular responsibility of parents to foster the religious life of their children, especially to see that they learn to pray. Children mostly relate quite naturally and unsentimentally to religion: they are still nearer to 'heaven,' and many parents, perhaps hesitant to pray themselves, learn to pray together with their children.

Even during the pregnancy it is good if the parents include the coming child in their prayers. The same applies to the unborn as to the departed: the thresholds between one existence and the next, whether of birth or death, are not a barrier. The child's soul perceives the kind of thoughts and feelings with which the parents live in their anticipation of the birth. Indeed, prayer forms an actual 'bridge,' enabling the child to have beneficent access to the human beings to whom it is about to entrust itself.

After the birth, the parents may pray for and over the child until it is old enough to join in the prayer. One of the most essential things we can give our children for their later life is that we also help them to make the Lord's Prayer their own.

Grace before meals

Saying grace before a meal has become rather unfashionable because most people can no longer see the point of it. Here, too, we can learn from children to renew this custom. Once they have got to know a grace, children ask for it. We cannot go into long and detailed justifications for saying grace, but we can at least remind ourselves that although the realm of nutrition has been thoroughly researched, the great mystery remains as to how material, physical nourishment is transformed to become our body and our blood. When we say grace, we accompany this process, so fundamental to our earthly existence, with feelings of reverence and thankfulness.

> *The plant roots quicken in the night of the earth,*
> *The leaves unfold through the might of the air,*
> *The fruit ripens through the power of the sun.*
> *So quickens the soul in the shrine of the heart,*
> *And man's spirit unfolds in the light of the world,*
> *So ripens man's strength in the glory of God.*[*]
> Rudolf Steiner

Prayer when in distress

We have already considered the special character of prayer in the event of distress, in life-threatening situations etc. In such circumstances, a direct appeal to God in a sort of instantaneous, impulsive prayer seems quite justified. If we have already formed a close bond with the Lord's Prayer, its power will also prove valuable here. If there is time, the whole prayer may be said, otherwise just a sentence or two, or even single words.

It not uncommon for people to wake up in the middle of the night with a feeling of deep anxiety. It can then be helpful to speak the Lord's Prayer aloud, and perhaps several times in succession until the anxiety subsides. The Lord's Prayer, spoken aloud, also provides protection if one feels threatened spiritually in some way.

[*] From M. Jones, *Prayers and Graces* (Floris Books).

Conclusion

On reading this book, it may sometimes have been felt that certain statements in it could have done with more clarification, perhaps even justification. That is unfortunately unavoidable in a booklet of this size. There are suggestions for further reading, where more detailed explanations can be found. Everything in this little book is simply presented as suggestions and help to find our own, personal approach to prayer.

Finally, here are some pertinent words by Rudolf Steiner from his lecture, *On the Nature of Prayer.*

You will sometimes hear it said: 'What difference can it possibly make to the course of the world if we pray for this or that? After all, the world runs according to fixed laws that we cannot change!'

Now, anyone who really wants to get to know a power must seek it in its right place. We have looked for the power of prayer in the human soul and have found it to be something that advances the soul. And anyone who knows that it is the Spirit that works in the world, and that the human soul is part of the realm of the Spirit, will also know that not only material forces operate in the world according to external laws; rather, everything of the nature of spiritual beings has effects in the world, even though the effects of these powers and beings are not visible to the outer eye or to materialistic science. So if we strengthen our spiritual life through prayer, all we have to do is wait for the effects. They will not fail to come. But only those who themselves have become aware of the reality of the power of prayer will look for the effect of prayer in the external world.

Anyone who has recognized this can make the following experiment: having scorned the power of prayer for ten years, let him look back on this ten-year period in which he has

*been living without praying; and then look back on another
ten-year period, also in the past, in which he had become
aware of the power of prayer. Now let him compare these two
decades. He will see how the course of his life changed under
the influence of the power that flowed into his soul through
and with the prayer. Powers reveal themselves through their
effects. It is easy to deny the existence of powers and forces if
one does not even attempt to call up their effect. No one has
the right to refute the power of prayer who has not so much as
given prayer a chance to work in the soul. Or are we to think
that those who have never developed or approached the power
of light, can know it?* A power that is to work in the soul and
through the soul can only be recognized when it is put to use.

Verses and Prayers

Asking among people
for the greatest of miracles, I found:
that there was no earth,
nor heaven above,
that there was neither tree or mountain,
and animals none,
no sun that shone,
no gleaming moon,
nor the mighty sea.

Though there was nothing
from end to end,
yet there was the One almighty God,
the most compassionate of beings,
and there were with him
many divine spirits.

God almighty,
who hast made heaven and earth,
and hast given human beings so much good,
give me in your grace
true faith and good will,
wisdom, insight and strength
to resist the Devil
to ward off evil,
and actively to do your will.

Wessobrunner Prayer, ninth century

Lord, make me an instrument of Thy peace:
that where there is hatred I may bring love,
that where there is insult I may bring pardon,
that where there is strife I may bring harmony,
that where there is error I may bring truth,
that where there is doubt I may bring faith,
that where there is despair I may bring hope,
that where there is darkness I may bring light,
that where there is sorrow I may bring joy.
Let me learn to comfort rather than be comforted,
Let me learn to understand rather than be understood,
Let me learn to love rather than be loved.
For it is by giving that one receives,
It is by self-forgetting that one finds,
It is by forgiving that one is forgiven,
It is by dying that one awakens to eternal life.

Francis of Assisi (1182–1226)

Recommended reading

William Barclay, *The Plain Man looks at the Lord's Prayer*, Collins, Glasgow.

—, *The Master's Men*, Collins, Glasgow.

Adam Bittleston, *Meditative Prayers for Today*, Floris, Edinburgh.

—, *Loneliness*, Floris, Edinbugh.

—, *Our Spiritual Companions*, Floris, Edinbugh.

Emil Bock, *The Rhythm of the Christian Year*, Floris, Edinburgh.

Evelyn Capel, *The Christian Year*, Floris, Edinbugh.

Alexander Carmichael (Ed.), *Carmina Gadelica, Hymns and Incantations*, Floris, Edinburgh.

Stanley Drake, *Though You Die*, Floris, Edinburgh.

Rudolf Frieling, *The Hope of the World, Contemplations and Aphorisms*, Floris, Edinburgh.

—, *New Testament Studies*, Floris, Edinburgh.

Sarah Johnson, *Daring to be Different*, Darton, Longman & Todd, London.

Michael Jones (Ed.), *Prayers and Graces*, Floris, Edinburgh.

Jon Madsen (Trans.), *The New Testament, Floris*, Edinburgh.

Friedrich Rittelmeyer, *Meditation*, Floris, Edinburgh.

Hans-Werner Schroeder, *The Christian Creed*, Floris, Edinburgh.

—, *The Trinity* Floris, Edinburgh.

Rudolf Steiner, *Breathing the Spirit, Meditations for Times of Day and Season of the Year*, Steiner Press, Forest Row.

—, *Christianity as Mystical Fact*, Steiner Press, Forest Row.

—, *Knowledge of Higher Worlds*, Steiner Press, Forest Row.

—, *Christ and the Human Soul*, Steiner Press, Forest Row.

—, *The Nature of Praying* Steiner Press, Forest Row.

—, *Religion: an Introductory Reader*, Ed. Andrew Welburn, Steiner Press, Forest Row.

—, *The Lord's Prayer, an Esoteric Study*, Steiner Press, Forest Row.

—, *Life after Death*, Steiner Press, Forest Row.